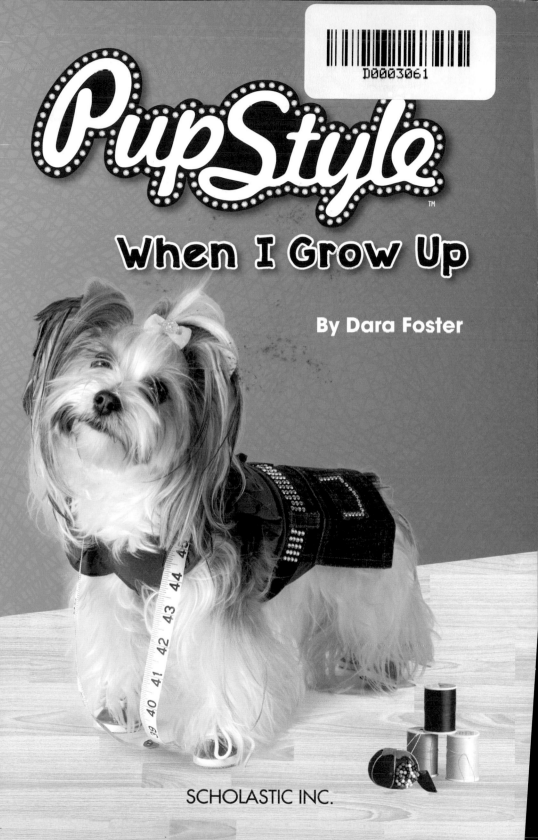

PupStyle

When I Grow Up

By Dara Foster

SCHOLASTIC INC.

I dedicate this book to my daughters, Parker and Ripley.

A very special "thank you" to Melissa Gampbel at doggiecoutureshop.com for supplying the pet fashions and accessories to make this book a reality.

Pet fashion styling, dog model casting, photo shoot production, and art direction by Dara Foster.
Assistant pet fashion styling and casting by Parker Spooner.
Photography by Mats Rudels.

Credits:
Front cover, title page, p. 43: dog model Betony, top by East Side Collection, skirt by Dog In The Closet, shoes by JML; p. 7: dog model Cosmo, firefighter costume by Pam Pet, shoes by Doggy Style Designs; p. 11: dog model Baby Howard; p. 15: dog model Petey, surgeon costume by Beth Kramer; p. 19: dog model Oscar Madison; p. 23: dog model Captain, shirt by Gidget-Gear by Tiki, necktie by Mirage Pets, pants by Gidget-Gear by Tiki; p. 27: dog model Charlie; p. 31: dog model Snarf, aviator hat by Dogo, bomber jacket by Roxy & Lulu; p. 35: dog model Lily, police officer costume by Rubies, shoes by Pet Edge-Guardian Gear; p. 39: dog model Bebe, plaid shirt by Worthy Dog, jeans by Puppy Love; p. 47: dog model Gia, dress by Hip Doggie, shoes by DS Doggy Style Design; p.51: dog model Star, beret by Barking Baby; p.55: dog model Oliver, shirt and blazer by Gidget-Gear by Tiki, necktie by Mirage Pet Products; p. 59: dog model Owen, overalls by Klippo, shirt by Worthy Dog, shoes by DS Doggy Style Designs; p. 63: dog model Trixie, shirt by Gidget-Gear by Tiki, bowtie by Penny and Poe.
Backgrounds/other photos: cover floor: first_emotion/Thinkstock; cover top right: PeopleImages/iStockphoto; back cover top: FangXiaNuo/iStockphoto; back cover center background: diane555/iStockphoto; 1 floor: first_emotion/Thinkstock; 3: damedeeso/Thinkstock; 5: kali9/iStockphoto; 7 background: asantosg/ iStockphoto; 9: Cathy Yeulet/Thinkstock; 11 background: macrovector/Thinkstock; 13: FangXiaNuo/ iStockphoto; 15: diane555/iStockphoto; 17: NASA; 19 background: Sahua/Dreamstime; 21: simonkr/ iStockphoto; 23 background: alla_snesar/iStockphoto; 25: Wavebreakmedia Ltd/Thinkstock; 27 background: valery_green/iStockphoto; 29: IPGGutenbergUKLtd/iStockphoto; 31 airport: mightyisland/iStockphoto; 31 plane: RedlineVector/iStockphoto; 33 background: Publicimage/Dreamstime; 33: Siri Stafford/Thinkstock; 35 background: bluebearry/iStockphoto; 37: Yuri_Arcurs/iStockphoto; 39 floor: CG Textures; 39 desk: djvstock/iStockphoto; 41: PeopleImages/iStockphoto; 43 floor: first_emotion/Thinkstock; 45: Jetta Productions/ Thinkstock; 47 background: adekvat/iStockphoto; 49: Antonio_Diaz/Thinkstock; 51 floor: filo/iStockphoto; 53: Ratz Attila/Dreamstime; 55 background: bakhtiar_zein/Dreamstime; 57: tunart/iStockphoto; 59 background: Youst/iStockphoto; 61: PeopleImages/iStockphoto; 63 background: Designed by Freepik.

ISBN 978-1-338-10540-7

10 9 8 7 6 5 4 3 2 1   17 18 19 20 21

Printed in Malaysia   106
First printing, September 2017

Book design by Marissa Asuncion

There are about 340 breeds of dogs in the world. That's a lot of pups! There are even more types of jobs and careers. But not every dog or job is right for everyone. Flip the page to learn about some incredible careers and see some adorable dogs!

FIREFIGHTER

Firefighters have a very dangerous job. They rescue people from fires and other accidents or emergencies. They use lots of tools while they work, including hoses, axes, and ladders. When firefighters are on the job, they must be ready to help people at any time—even in the middle of the night!

CHIWEENIE

Firefighters used to have another important tool—dogs! Before firefighters had fire engines, they used horses to pull their equipment. Dogs, specifically Dalmatians, were used to clear a path in the streets and protect the horses in case they were spooked by the fire. That is why many firehouses today still have a firehouse dog!

CONSTRUCTION WORKER

Construction workers build roads, buildings, and bridges—and they can help to tear them down, too! Sometimes they carry belts with small tools like hammers and wrenches. Other times, construction workers use bigger tools. They use large machines called bulldozers to move dirt and dig deep holes.

BULLDOG

Dogs dig holes, too, but usually just in the backyard! Some dogs dig because a shallow hole keeps them cool in the summer heat. Other dogs use the holes to bury their favorite toy or bone to keep it safe. Some dogs dig holes just because they have lots of fun doing it!

DOCTOR

Doctors have very important jobs. They examine sick patients, discover what's wrong with them, and work to fix it. There are different doctors for every part of the body. Some doctors examine eyes. Some specialize in brains or hearts. But every doctor's job is to help his or her patients!

YORKSHIRE TERRIER

Someday doctors may get a little canine help! Scientists have discovered special sensors in the back of dogs' noses that can help detect if a patient has a disease like cancer. Maybe one day doctors will have dogs in the examining room to lend a paw!

ASTRONAUT

The United States formed NASA in 1958. In 1969, NASA sent the first astronauts to walk on the moon! It is tough to become an astronaut. Astronauts must be in good physical shape and have a college degree in math or science. Some astronauts even need experience flying a jet. Less than 400 people have ever become NASA astronauts!

DACHSHUND

One step for dogkind? Laika the astronaut dog launched into space in 1957. She was the first creature to ever orbit Earth! Now human astronauts have spent more than a year in space in one visit! The research and work that astronauts have done have helped humans understand Earth and outer space.

AUTHOR

It's easy to curl up with a good book. But becoming an author who *writes* books requires a lot of practice. Countless dogs have been featured as main characters in popular books like *Old Yeller* and *Because of Winn-Dixie*. Authors draw inspiration from their favorite pups, proving that often they like to "write about what they know"!

BRUSSELS GRIFFON

Dogs love a good story, too! As part of the Shelter Buddies reading program, young kids read books to furry friends. This helps kids sharpen their reading skills, and it's a ton of fun for the pups, too. Shy dogs spend quality time with kids, which helps prepare the dogs for their new owners.

CHEF

It is hard work to become a good chef. Chefs have to plan menus, pick out yummy fresh ingredients, and then cook up delicious meals. They often go to special cooking schools before they begin working in restaurants. The best cooks can become head chefs at fancy restaurants and even participate in competitions.

GOLDEN RETRIEVER

Dogs love food! Pets will often beg for human food from their owners' plates during meals. But that doesn't mean they should be given any scraps! Dogs have special food and treats that are just right for them. There are even doggy bakeries! They make dog treats in lots of yummy flavors like peanut butter and pumpkin.

PILOT

American pilots have to train for 1,500 hours before they can fly a commercial plane. As the captain of the plane, the pilot guides the aircraft safely to its destination. A flight can be only a couple of minutes or take over sixteen hours! The biggest airplane can fit more than 850 people.

SHIH TZU

On most airlines, only a few dogs are allowed on each flight. The dogs must be under a certain weight and be kept in a crate during the flight. But there is also an all-pet airline so dogs no matter how big or small can fly "first class"!

POLICE OFFICER

Police officers have very important jobs. They investigate crimes, protect people and property, and help in emergency situations. In order to become a police officer, recruits attend Police Academy, where they learn skills to use on the job. Once they graduate, police officers patrol communities to keep them safe from crime.

MINIATURE SCHNAUZER

Sometimes police officers need a little help. Dogs' powerful ears and noses make them very valuable to police. They can find hidden evidence. Bomb-sniffing dogs can help protect people by smelling and finding dangerous chemicals. And sometimes dogs can even use their noses to help police track down missing people.

POLICE

SOFTWARE DEVELOPER

These days, almost anything can be done with the power of technology. Software developers create computer programs and smartphone apps for just about everything. Some apps are for playing games or music. Others are great for taking photos or chatting with friends. There's an app out there for everyone!

MALTIPOO

There are even special apps for dog owners! Dog lovers can download apps that pair dogs with new families. Other apps are great for training new puppies, finding a vet, tracking walks, or finding lost dogs. Pet owners can also use different apps to find dog sitters and set up a play date with other dogs nearby!

FASHION DESIGNER

Fashion designers are creative people who design clothing, shoes, and other accessories. Sometimes designers hold fashion shows where models walk the latest fashions down the runway. Their designs might appear in magazines or other fancy photo shoots. Other times, a designer's creations will go into stores across the country for people to buy!

BIEWER TERRIER

Some designers make clothes for dogs, too. One famous doggy clothing designer even had models present his clothes during a show at the famous New York Fashion Week! Dogs can wear all the hottest styles, just like humans. Coats, shoes, hats, dresses, and even bow ties—there's fashion for any doggy occasion!

TEACHER

Teachers have one of the most important jobs in the world. They teach students of all ages about all sorts of subjects. Some teachers help students learn science or reading, while others teach things like music and art. Many teachers work at schools and colleges, but a teacher can work anywhere students are ready to learn!

POMERANIAN

Dogs can be great students, too. Some dogs have teachers, or trainers, who help them learn to behave. Most dogs are trained when they are just puppies. Dogs usually learn to sit, stay, and roll over. But some dogs learn other tricks, too, like fetching the newspaper or jumping through hoops.

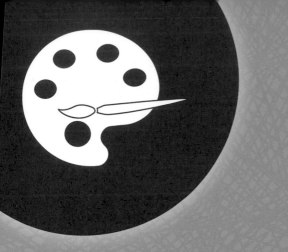

ARTIST

An artist is anyone who follows his or her creativity, like painters, musicians, or actors. Some art can be found in a museum, while other art is heard on the radio or seen on the stage or big screen. It takes a lot of dedication and practice to be an artist—but just a little imagination!

PIT BULL

Art isn't just for humans—dogs like it, too! In 2016, there was an art show in London that had artwork just for dogs. There are also many talented dog artists. Usually, a dog holds a paintbrush in its mouth and signs its work with a paw print. Humans can't get enough of these colorful doggy paintings!

NEWSCASTER

Newscasters report the news on television. People everywhere tune into news shows each day to find out what is happening around the world. For every report, newscasters cover many different topics, from international politics to local weather. Sometimes newscasters interview special guests or talk to reporters who are "on the scene" of a breaking story.

PAPILLON

Humans aren't the only ones on TV. Sometimes dogs make the news, too! In 2014, newscasters on all the top news shows told the story of an incredible dog named Major. When Major saw his owner was in trouble, he dialed 911 with his paws. This heroic dog saved his owner's life! What a story!

FARMER

A farmer is responsible for operating a farm. A farm can be acres large or it can be in the farmer's backyard. Farmers on large farms can plant crops like wheat, corn, or pumpkins. Other farmers raise animals like cows or chickens. Some do both! But many farms have tons of different animals like sheep, horses, and pigs.

PUG

A farm dog has a very important job. Because dogs have such a good sense of direction, they can help guide other animals, like sheep, to where they need to go. There are twenty to thirty different breeds of herding dogs. Size doesn't matter with these dogs. Some small dogs herd much larger animals like cows!

SCIENTIST

From dinosaurs to lightbulbs to computers, scientists have made incredible discoveries throughout history. There are so many topics for scientists to study that a scientist usually picks a certain area, or specialty, to focus on. Scientists study things like Earth, space, and human behavior. There are even scientists who are dog experts!

DACHSHUND–SKYE TERRIER

Some special dogs become service animals. They help people who are visually or hearing impaired. Other service dogs keep their owners calm in situations where they might be nervous. Dogs are so dependable and loyal that scientists have discovered that a dog can even copy its owner's behavior. That means when its owner is sad, the dog may act sad, too.

There are so many dogs and jobs out there, it can be hard to choose just one! When a family is choosing a dog or when an adult is picking a career, it's important to do lots of research to find the right fit. There is a different dog and a different job for everyone!